LYRICS OF LIFE AND LOVE

DATE DUE

DEMCO 38-296

WILLIAM STANLEY BRAITHWAITE

LYRICS
OF LIFE AND LOVE

BY

WILLIAM STANLEY BRAITHWAITE

AYER COMPANY, PUBLISHERS, INC.
SALEM, NEW HAMPSHIRE 03079

Copyright 1904 *By*

ER & COMPANY

tember 1904

on, 1988
lishers, Inc.
reet
hire 03079

ISBN 0-88143-081-1

First Mnemosyne reprinting 1969

**Reprinted from a copy in the
Fisk University Library Negro Collection.**

Copyright © 1969   Mnemosyne Publishing Co., Inc.   Miami, Florida

Library of Congress Catalog Card Number:
70-88540

Printed in the United States of America

FOR permission to reprint several pieces in this volume acknowledgment is due to the Christian Endeavor Herald, National Magazine, Colored American Magazine, Howard Spectator, and others.

CONTENTS

CONTENTS — (*Continued*)

TO MY MOTHER

LYRICS OF LIFE AND LOVE

RHAPSODY

I AM glad daylong for the gift of song,
    For time and change and sorrow;
For the sunset wings and the world-end things
    Which hang on the edge of to-morrow.
I am glad for my heart whose gates apart
    Are the entrance-place of wonders,
Where dreams come in from the rush and din
    Like sheep from the rains and thunders.

OUT OF THE SILENCE OF MY DREAMS

I HEAR a voice that speaks to me
　　Out of the silence of my dreams;
Somewhere from long eternity
　　Where the first white dawn gleams.

Night and the stars, day and the sun,
　　Winds and the trumpets of mid-seas,
All in one common key they run
　　Through deathless melodies.

Take this, my answer for all time —
　　Yea, to his speech, to his command:
Surrendering all life of mine
　　Unto his heart and hand.

DIVIDED

'TIS strange that we should fall apart
    And live divided nights and days!
What loneliness crowds on the heart,
    What vacancy in eyes that gaze.

Oh! if there were a little child,
    Whose innocence had made it wise,
Remembrance would have reconciled
    Its father's face, its mother's eyes.

TO A PERSIAN ROSE

To E. A. B.

IN the world's garden close,
    Where a wild Eden blows,
Where the earth's treasury
Hoards by the Arat sea,
    You grew, a rose.

In the flushed lyric dawn,
Poignant with scented heat,
Gold dew you fed upon,
Gleaming like crystals — sweet
    Stars of the lawn.

From all the islands blent,
One thousand essences,
Odors of ravishment
Culled from the Eastern seas
    Filled you with scent.

All the East's lavishness
Dowered and nurtured you,
Till past all loveliness
That the East ever knew,
    Regal you grew.

One June in Maenad-mirth
The great luxurious Mother
Gave you strange, mystic birth,—
Such as she gave no other —
    You child of earth.

No unguent was too precious
For the high gods to give;
No passion too delicious
Through which you might not live,
    To joy and grieve.

Long wanton centuries since,
In days of Rome and Tyre,
Thou mated once a prince
Of a great Persian sire
    For Love's desire.

O thou wast more than fair!
Thou Rose of Paradise —
In lips, and cheeks, and hair,—
All beauty wonder-wise
    'Neath those hot skies.

A DREAM AND A SONG
To B. V. T.

A DREAM comes in and a song goes forth;
The wind is south and the sun is north —
The daisies run on the dunes to the sea,
And over the world my soul goes free.

Ah, over the world to sing and roam
In the sun and wind — without a home
Till a woman's heart shall dream and say:
"O song of the dreamer I bid you stay

And sing in my heart: make glad my feet
To run as the winds do, soft and fleet
Over the dunes and down to the sea,
Where Love came home in a dream to me."

TWO QUESTIONS

HEART of the soft, wild rose
 Hid in a forest close
Far from the world away,
Sweet for a night and day.
Rose, is it good to be sweet,
Sun and the dews to greet?

Life that is mine to keep
In travail, play and sleep
Firm on a tossing ball,
Drilled to march at a call;
Work, love, death — these three —
Life, is there more for me?

A LITTLE SONG
To T. E. S.

A LITTLE song ill worth your while
On which to waste more than a smile,
Alas, I sing, for love is long —
A little song.

Though life be brief and art outlive
What joy or sorrow earth may give,
Time, then, might let the years prolong
A little song.

And it may chance your face will turn
Some day, the singer to discern —
Yea, smile to see who sang so long,
A little song.

JAMES RUSSELL LOWELL

STEEPT in the Muses' youthful, sultry maze,
    He linkt his own with Shakespeare's lucid
        days —
And Camelot came to Cambridge in his heart,
Where Rosaline met ancient Britomart.

IF I COULD TOUCH

IF I could touch your hand to-night
   And hear you speak one little word,
I then might understand your flight
   Up the star steps, unseen, unheard.

If through the mists of gold and gray
   That tint the weary sunset skies,
There shone two stars across the bay
   That thrilled me like your passionate eyes—

If only some small part of you
   Would speak, or touch, or rise in sight,
Death would be then between us two
   The passing of a summer's night.

EVENING

AT my window what delight
 Here to sit and watch the night,
Stealing after fleeting day,
Soft and quiet all the way.
Through my window like a flute's
Comes the robin's dying notes,
While above me dim and far
Silent breaks the evening star.

At my window o'er the street,
In the twilight calm and sweet,
From dim vistas of the past
Dreams come to me thick and fast;
Some are clothed in bright array,
Phantoms of a happier day —
Some, wan spectral shades assume,
Draped in anguished hours of doom.

This brief span of years we lease
Gives us fewer hours of peace
Than it does of strife and toil —
Therefore when subsides the broil,
Let it be but one brief hour,
'Tis a providential dower,
Just a stop upon the road
Easing us of life's great load.

So to-night is one of those
Blissful times of blest repose;
And in unison I seem
With night's universal dream.
All is quiet near and far
From the lily to the star,
And my soul in dreamy ease
Strikes the soothing chords of peace.

A LEAVE-TAKING, I

LET there be one word more
 Before you go —
Some sweet old thing
Remembering,
Alas to know —
Some hope you fed, some look you gave,
Dead now in love's deep grave.

So, speak — and then depart,
And I will keep
The best of you forever in my heart.
All else shall sleep
As if death came and taught them to forget.
Only the best
Of you shall live without regret,
Within my breast.

YOUR hand in mine for a space,
    Through a brief living sigh;
The red rose white in your face,
    And a swift good-bye.

One moment! ah, could it be
    Life's veriest depth and height!
The death of my soul for me —
    And you — well, the red rose white.

KEATS WAS AN UNBELIEVER

" Keats was not a believer "
— *Biographical Sketch*

" **K**EATS was an unbeliever," — so they
read.
The critic's words defame the poet's soul:
Nature and Life as one stupendous whole
He traced to the source. Thereof a Fountain-
head:
His worship was where light enshrined the **head**
Of Beauty:— for true love and wisdom stole
From God to man within her aureole,
And God's elect but followed where she lead.

Of God's elect was Keats: his earthly duty
To sing again the music of **creation**;
That first of all, God's dream of life was Beauty;
That Beauty is the seed of all salvation:—
Holiest of all unbelievers, thus,
He made " Believing " possible for us.

THE WATCHERS

TWO women on the lone wet strand
    (The wind's out with a will to roam)
The waves wage war on rocks and sand,
    (And a ship is long due home.)

The sea sprays in the women's eyes —
    (Hearts can writhe like the sea's wild foam)
Lower descend the tempestuous skies,
    (For the wind's out with a will to roam.)

"O daughter, thine eyes be better than mine,"
    (The waves ascend high as yonder dome)
"North or south is there never a sign?"
    (And a ship is long due home.)

They watched there all the long night through —
    (The wind's out with a will to roam)
Wind and rain and sorrow for two,—
    (And heaven on the long reach home.)

IN A GRAVE-YARD

IN calm fellowship they sleep
   Where the graves are dark and **deep,**
Where nor hate nor fraud nor feud
Mar their perfect brotherhood.

After all was done they went
Into dreamless sleep, content,
That the years would pass them by,
Sightless, soundless, where they lie.

Wines and roses, song and dance,
Have no portion in their trance —
The four seasons are as one,
Dark of night, and light of sun.

THE LAND OF HOPE-TO-BE

THERE'S a way to happiness
 Up the road of Dreams,
Where my soul goes wayfaring
 By the sleepy streams.

Heart that sends your memories
 In the shape of song,
To the land of Hope-to-Be,
 Is the journey long?

Nay, companion of my house,
 In the longest flight,
Distance in desire is drowned
 As the day in night.

Heart and soul go wayfaring
 Up the road of Dreams,
To the land of Hope-to-Be
 By the sleepy streams.

A CITY GARDEN

HID in a close and lowly nook
　　In a city yard where no grass grows —
Wherein nor sun, nor stars may look
　　Full-faced, — are planted three short rows
　　Of pansies, geraniums, and a rose.

A little girl with quiet, wide eyes,
　　Slender figured, in tattered gown,
Whose pallored face no country skies
　　Have quickened to a healthy brown,
　　Made this garden in the barren town.

Poor little flowers, your life is hard:
　　No sun, nor wind, nor evening dew.
Poor little maid, whose city yard
　　Is a world of happy dreams to you —
　　God grant some day your dreams come true.

SEA LYRIC

OVER the seas to-night, love,
    Over the darksome deeps,
Over the seas to-night, love,
    Slowly my vessel creeps.
Over the seas to-night, love,
    Waking the sleeping foam —
Sailing away from thee, love,
    Sailing from thee and home.
Over the seas to-night, love,
    Dreaming beneath the spars —
Till in my dreams you shine, love,
    Bright as the listening stars.

DISTANCES

JUST where that star above
　　Shines with a cold, dispassionate smile —
If in the flesh I'd travel there,
　　How many, many a mile!

If this, my soul, should be
　　Unprisoned from its earthly bond,
Time could not count its markless flight
　　Beyond that star, beyond!

SONG

UP and down the beach I wander
   Here to-night beside the sea,
In my ears the ocean-thunder,
   In my heart the dreams of thee.
      The sea, the sea is high, love,
      Dark, dark, O dark, the sky, love,
      And sad is my heart.

In thy outward journey passing
   Through the narrow gates of night,
Was there travail in the massing
   Of the waters void of light?
      O the sea, the sea is high, love,
      Swift surge the waters by, love,
      And sad is my heart.

AN OLD DREAM

YOU sang that song beside an olden sea,
   In some low dream, some hundred years
      ago;
The time, the place is all unknown to me —
   It is the feeling in my heart I know.
We were two Grecians then, I do believe,
   And caught a dream some fair god's passion
      sighed;
Time wandered far, and left our hearts to
      grieve —
   But somewhere Love lived on, though all else
      died.

Dear, as you sing, it all comes back to me;
   The mood, though filled with centuries of
      strife
Is the same ecstasy; only the sea
   Seems grown a little weary of its life.
No change has come unto your voice and heart,
   No shadow on your face; and in your eyes —
Though Time has kept them from my eyes
      apart —
   The rapture of sea-dreams and memories.

LOVE IS A STAR

THIS is the song I sing for you,
  Out of my heart the melodies rise —
Life is long for the brave and true,
  Love is a star to your faithful eyes.

This is the dream your heart must hold:
  One in the world is faithful still —
Here is warmth from the wind and cold,
  Here is rest from the sea and hill.

ON A PRESSED FLOWER IN MY COPY OF KEATS

AS Keats' old honeyed volume of romance
     I oped to-day to drink its Latmos air,
I found all pressed a white flower lying where
The shepherd lad watched Pan's herd slow advance.
Ah, then what tender memories did chance
To bring again the day, when from your hair,
This frail carnation, delicate and fair,
You gave me, that I now might taste its trance.
And so to-day it brings a mellow dream
Of that sweet time when but to hear you speak
Filled all my soul. What waves of passion seem
About this flower to linger and to break,
Lit by the glamor of the moon's pale beam
The while my heart weeps for this dear flower's sake.

WHEN TWILIGHT COMES WITH DREAMS

O LET the music play a little longer,
  And sweetheart clasp me closer to your
      breast.
Life is strong, and death; but love is stronger —
  And sweeter, sweeter, rest.

Oh, sweet is rest when love is watching over,
  And twilight comes with dreams that reassure;
Weaving out of the silences that hover
  Hopes which must endure.

THE DEPARTURE OF PIERROTT

WE have housed, my Columbine,
　　With our songs and books and dreams,
　Quiet and content it seems
Through the winter's cloud and shine.

In our little attic room
　Looking o'er the city square,
　Quite outside the world of care,
All unaltered by its gloom, —

Thou and I, my Columbine,
　Let the world of men below
　Unacquainted come and go,
In secludedness divine.

Ah, those nights, so long, were sweet,
　And we shall not soon forget
　Love songs sung in a duet,
Far above the city street.

And the company 'twas ours
　To abide in — Tennyson,
　Shelley, Keats, and Emerson —
Joyed us in those winter hours.

So, my Columbine, together
  We lived the long season through
  Till March came, whose wild winds blew
Us to days of April weather.

All the first sweet dreams of Spring
  Born again of new desires,
  In me light unquenching fires
To be up and wandering.

Newer hopes have won my trust —
  I but answer to the call,
  April smiling over all
Fills my soul with wander-lust.

There is magic in the stir
  When our mother April wakes;
  Some wild riot in me breaks
When I feel the pulse of her.

On the slowly greening slopes
  Something in the hanging haze,
  Luring, leads my tramping ways
On a quest for April Hopes.

Nature keeps an open house,
  I am bidden to her board;
  And she fills me from her hoard
Where the sons of earth carouse.

LOUISBERG SQUARE

A QUIET little space, set in
  Upon the sloping hillside, where
Comes not the sound of traffic's din
  To fill the air.

The stately houses on each side,
  The little park which lies between —
How in seclusion, all abides
  A quiet dream.

APRIL

A T morn when light mine eyes unsealed
    I gazed upon the open field;
The rain had fallen in the night —
The landscape in the new day's light
A countenance of grace revealed
Upon the meadow, wood and height.

The sun's light was a smile of gold,
Ere shut by sudden fold on fold
Of surging, showering clouds from view;
No sooner hid than it broke through
A tearful smile upon the wold
Where earth reflected heaven's blue.

Each separate divided part
Of day, was as the threefold art
Of God, who dreamed three dreams and made
The morning, noon, and night parade
In ever changing guise athwart
The day's hours, in His dreams arrayed.

The sky was as a canvas spun
To paint the new spring's nocturns on ;
A blended melody of tints —
The sea's hue, and the myriad hints
Of garden-closes, when the sun
Hath stamped the work of nature's mints.

OUT OF THE SUNSET'S RED

OUT of the sunset's red
    Into the blushing sea,
The winds of day drop dead
    And dreams come home to me. —
The sea is still, — and apart
Is a stillness in my heart.

The night comes up the beach,
    The dark steals over all,
Though silence has no speech
    I hear the sea-dreams call
To my heart; — and in reply
It answers with a sigh.

TWILIGHT AND DREAMS

A T the outer edge of the world,
 Where the long grey mists arise,
Between the sunset and the sea
 I gaze with longing eyes.

O the twilight and dreams for me,
 And the things my fancy paints —
My hopes the light upon the sea
 Which slowly faints and faints.

The surge and beat of the sea,
 The mournful and endless dole, —
They swell with a thousand questionings
 And overflow my soul.

LOVE'S WAYFARING

D^O you remember, love —
        How long ago it seems —
When by the pebbled cove,
    Our sweet, fair dreams
Took wing?

Alas, how long it is —
    What wasted years between;
What untouched hours of bliss;
    And unlived dream —
Time's sting!

Were not the high tides sweet!
    The sails upon the stream —
The billows' bounding beat,
    The sea-gull's scream
And swing.

What murmuring music rose
    From zephyr's low-tuned chords,
To which in love's repose
    Our hearts made words
To sing.

Ah, sweet, where is Love gone?
  To what bourne, east or west,
Shall you and I alone
  Bide his behest
Wand'ring ?

SHE SLEEPS BENEATH THE WINTER SNOW

SHE sleeps beneath the winter snow
    In Cedar's wintry vale;
The winter stars above her shine,
    The pines about her wail,
And icy winds do chill and blow.
    My Ciceline, my Ciceline,
        Sleeps deep and low
        Beneath the snow.

I sit beside my fire bright
    And watch the embers glow,
And yet to-night so dark and chill
    She sleeps beneath the snow.
And though the place be hid from sight,
My dreams its gloomy darkness fill —
    With Ciceline's my heart is low
    Beneath the winter snow.

LYRIC: WHEN THE STILL SOMBRE
EVENING CLOSES DOWN

WHEN the still, sombre evening closes down
  Amid the autumn preludes of the wood,
 I feel my soul take on its dreamy mood
'Midst nature's gold and brown.

The dear old dreams of June — blue-bird and
   rose
  Have sunk into these sadder phantasies,
  And once again old buried memories
Wake from their long repose.

Ah, when I look on Hesper clear and bright,
  The thought of one dear autumn, sad and cool,
  Transports me to a bygone forest pool
One long gone autumn night.

Now that my vision brightens, memory brings
  That forest opening — sere leaves, the sheen
  Of moonlight which soft stole the leaves be-
   tween
In their down flutterings.

How solemn was the scene — that solitude!
　　Those fulgent woods our holy marriage house
　　Where Zephyrus sang his choral through the
　　　　boughs
To bless us where we stood.

Ah, memory! dear conjurer of tears!
　　Bring vividly the vision of that night,
　　When our two hearts pledged by kind nature's
　　　　rite
A union through the years.

CHILD ELSIE

FOR love of the sea, Child Elsie,
  Untethered the dory's rope,
To ride with native impulse
  The water's rise and slope.

For love of the seaman's maiden,
  The mew-tides running down,
Swept out to sea the dory
  Afar from the fishing town.

A SEA-PRAYER

LORD of wind and water
    Where the ships go down
Reaching to the sunrise,
Lifting like a crown,

Out of the deep-hidden
Wells of night and day —
Mind the great sea-farers
On the open way.

When the last lights darken
On the far coastline,
Wave and port and peril
Sea-Lord — all are thine.

IT WERE AS IF THIS WORLD WERE PARADISE

IT were as if this world were Paradise,
  That little hour when by the dancing sea
I told thee of the love I had for thee.
There seemed a newer glory in the skies
When thou didst look with pitying sweet eyes
Upon me when I pleaded. I felt that we
Did balance in some mystic harmony
Of old rose-gardens and low ocean sighs.
The sunshine stole some glory from your hair:
The sea, the magic of your eyes of blue —
The grace of all your nature soft and fair
Fill'd all the world until an Eden grew;
You were a gracious Eve beside me there,
And all the world was Paradise with you.

YULE-SONG: A MEMORY

DECEMBER comes, snows come,
    Comes the wintry weather;
Faces from away come —
    Hearts must be together.
        Down the stair-steps of the hours
        Yule leaps the hills and towers —
    Fill the bowl and hang the holly,
    Let the times be jolly.

Day comes, and night comes
    And the guests assemble —
Once again the old dream comes
    That I would dissemble.
        Falls a shadow 'cross the floor,
        Seen! — and is seen no more.
    O that memory would forego
    The hanging of the Mistletoe.

VOICE OF THE SEA

VOICE of the sea that calls to me,
    Heart of the woods my own heart loves,
I am part of your mystery —
    Moved by the soul your own soul moves.

Dream of the stars in the night-sea's dome,
    Somewhere in your infinite space
After the years I will come home,
    Back to your halls to claim my place.

APRIL'S DREAM

THE stream's breath tastes of the wood's
      perfume,
Filled are the woods with foam:
And the sea like a sheet 'neath the summer noon,
    With the languorous swerve runs home.
The beat of a pulse the warm sun stirs
    In the air, the sea and stream,
Beckons the heart — and the soul allures
    Forth, into April's dream.

ON MUSIC

I CANNOT tell how high my soul takes
      wing,
  Nor to what depths in liquid sweets it sinks—
Yet well I know it suffers from thy sting,
  As one who of Cyceon mixture drinks.
And I can feel a rose-stream thro' me creep,
Curving about my senses, as they leap,
      And swell and rise and fall,
      As blossoms ambrosial
Shook from some full blown orange-tree in
    spring,
      Sink wav'ring to the ground
      And bound
Unto the zephyr's piping, in dizzy, dizzy ring!

SONG

OVER the long, the wide dark seas,
  Wandering, goes my dream,
Borne on winnowings of the breeze
High as the heavens seem.
And O, dear love, where the waters foam
  Further than pulsing star,
Wandering still my old dreams roam
Far from the shore — yea far!

THERE is music in the meadows, in the
air —
    Autumn is here;
Skies are gray, but hearts are mellow,
Leaves are crimson, brown, and yellow;
    Pines are soughing, birches stir,
And the Gipsy trail is fresh beneath the fir.

There is rhythm in the woods, and in the fields,
    Nature yields:
And the harvest voices crying,
Blend with Autumn zephyrs sighing;
    Tone and color, frost and fire,
Wings the nocturne Nature plays upon her lyre.

MOTHERHOOD

WITH what angelic countenance
    She wonders as she sits alone,
With tender fear, and musing glance
    Because a life is in her own.
Ah! if a woman should be loved
    'T is when she hears the silent voice,
'T is when an unknown life has moved
    Her soul to fear and to rejoice.
'T is when amidst life's blithesome scenes,
    A something speaks she cannot hear,
And quells her spirit till it dreams
    The sacred thing she is to bear.
Ah! what is needed most to bless
    The weary waiting of the time!
Love's duty rendered tireless
    To cheer her holy state sublime;
A tender presence that would teach
    Her more than laws of science could;
That, life belongs to each and each,
    To Fatherhood and Motherhood!

TO W. A. W. AND H. H.
on their Departure to Europe

GOOD-BYE, and may your journey be
    Through nights with pleasant stars
      above,
And may your days upon the sea
    Your souls with wonder fill and move.
By night the lyric-light of stars,
By day the pulsing tidal wars.

And may you safely reach the port
    Where sweet the old-world dreams repose
In garden, vale, and palace-court,
    Where long ago the sounds arose
Of feudal strife — and song took wing —
When men were brave, and Love was King.

And when you shall have made your stay
    Through summer-moons that filled and waned,
May westward autumn lead your way
    Untroubled, till your home is gained.
So may propitious fortune keep
And bring you safely o'er the deep.

THANKSGIVING

MY heart gives thanks for many things;
 For strength to labor day by day,
For sleep that comes when darkness wings
 With evening up the eastern way.
I give deep thanks that I'm at peace
 With kith and kin and neighbors, too —
Dear Lord, for all last year's increase,
 That helped me strive and hope and do.

My heart gives thanks for many things;
 I know not how to name them all.
My soul is free from frets and stings,
 My mind from creed and doctrine's thrall.
For sun and stars, for flowers and streams,
 For work and hope and rest and play —
For empty moments given to dreams,
 For these my heart gives thanks to-day.

LIFE AND DEATH

I RENTED once a house of clay,
  An object beautiful to see —
I lighted it with pleasant thoughts
  And Life 'twas named by Mystery.

And when long years therein I lived
  I moved into a fairer clime,
And then my house was named anew —
  For it was christened Death, by Time.

HOLLY BERRY AND MISTLETOE

THE trees are bare, wild flies the snow,
    Hearths are glowing, hearts are merry—
High in the air is the Mistletoe,
    Over the door is the Holly Berry.

Never have care how the winds may blow,
    Never confess the revel grows weary—
Yule is the time of the Mistletoe,
    Yule is the time of the Holly Berry.

WHEN I BID YOU GOOD-BYE AND GO

WHEN I bid you good-bye and go
  I do not want your tears to flow,
For I have filled so small a part
In your great heart.

And I shall sleep below and dream
You have been good to let it seem
I lived in all your heart — your life
Without one strife.

It cost so little — so, be kind
To keep a portion in your mind
Of me — remembering that I gave
Up to the grave.

DEAR heart, what tho' I press the heed-
  less throng
 While high the stars shine in their blue re-
  treat,
If so, I unto thee with heart of song
  Wend thro' the street.

Dear heart, what tho' my song's inaudible
 Unto this ceaseless, surging, heartless
  throng —
Far from the crowd wilt thou not hear it well
  All the night long?

BY AN INLAND LAKE

LONG drawn, the cool, green shadows
　　Steal o'er the lake's warm breast,
And the ancient silence follows
　　The burning sun to rest.

The calm of a thousand summers,
　　And dreams of countless Junes,
Return when the lake-wind murmurs
　　Thro' golden, August noons.

SONG

I WENT down the ways of the roses this
    noon,
The birds were in tune with the infinite skies,
And all my heart sang, " It is June, it is June,"
    And all my soul teemed with the lovely sur-
      prise,
As I went down the ways of the roses this noon.

And into my garden the shades bade them
    come,
    The wayfaring dreams that came forth of
      the sun :
" Come, rest," said the roses, " ere further ye
    roam ; "
    " Be my guests," said my heart, " till the day
      it be done,"
As into my garden the shades bade them come.

O long the dreams tarried within that sweet
    place,
    And unto my heart and the roses they told,
How on their long travel they met with a face
    All clouded with hair of the sun's fairest
      gold —
And my heart and the roses sighed in the sweet
    place.

SONG: TO-NIGHT THE STARS ARE WOOING, LOVE

TO-NIGHT the stars are wooing, love,
   The moon is full of languishment;
Low in the eastern firmament
Little, the golden waves above —
   My dreams are wand'ring pensive-wise
   Unto the bourne of echo-sighs
Beneath the stars, within the grove.

To-night the rose-leaves fell apart,
   And at their core the sweet dews dwell,
   While dreams of echo in the shell
Conjures the crimson-scented heart.
   So, love, thy sweet influence steals
   Upon me, and my spirit heals,
And dreams what loveliness thou art.

TO-NIGHT ACROSS THE SEA

TO-NIGHT I sent a dream across the sea,
　　Beyond the bourne where sky and water
　　　　meet;
Its ghost came back in mournful melody
　　Of waters at my feet.

The dream gone out, its ghost abides with me,
　　A visitant of sorrow in my heart;
And ever clings thereto the mystery
　　The mournful seas impart.

A MEMORY

MY heart to thee an answer makes,
 O long, slow whisper of the sea,
Whose charm of mournful music wakes
 A dream, a memory.

Touched hands, met lips, and soft fair speech —
 Soul's silence to the past replies,
When love and hope illumined each,
 Within a girl's blue eyes.

AFTER HARVEST

FAINT is the speech of the tired heart
  To the call of dreams replying,
When hope wends home across the fields
  Where the rose o' the year is dying.

O weary head and heart and hands
  Look up where the sun is dying —
Love leads you home across the fields
  To the call of dreams replying.

IT'S A LONG WAY

IT'S a long way the sea-winds blow
　　Over the sea-plains blue, —
But longer far has my heart to go
　　Before its dreams come true.

It's work we must, and love we must,
　　And do the best we may,
And take the hope of dreams in trust
　　To keep us day by day.

It's a long way the sea-winds blow —
　　But somewhere lies a shore —
Thus down the tide of Time shall flow
　　My dreams forevermore.

I BLOW YOU A KISS

I BLOW you a kiss on the evening wind
　My dear, wherever you be;
Up in the north or down in the south,
　Or over the rolling sea.

I blow you a kiss, but after the kiss
　Do you know what follows, my dear?
Something the wind cannot bring to you —
　Only a little tear.

SEA VOICES

O'ER the wintry sea,
    Mingled with its tone
Comes a voice to me,
    That's not the sea's own.

Low and soft it is,
    Near and far away —
Sad as winds that kiss
    The sea beyond the bay.

Soulless, restless, swell,
    O what radiant guest,
Sad, invisible,
    Hovers o'er thy breast?

Gray rocks and gray sea,
    Stretch of barren shore,
Grief and memory
    Claim me evermore.

TO ——

HALF in the dim light from the hall
    I saw your fingers rise and fall
Along the pale, dusk-shadowed keys,
And heard your subtle melodies.

The magic of your mastery leant
Your soul unto the instrument;
Strange-wise, its spell of power seemed
To voice the visions that you dreamed.

The music gave my soul such wings
As bore me through the shadowings
Of mortal bondage; flight on flight
I circled dreams' supremest height.

Above were tender twilight skies,
Where stars were dreams and memories —
The long forgotten raptures of
My youth's dead fires of hope and love.

IN MY LADY'S PRAISE

GOD wrought you flesh and hair and eyes
    From some immortal loom and dyes;
For thou art filled with every rare
And precious thing of earth, sky, air.
The magical blue of warm June skies
Gleams in your calm and sultry eyes;
The unguent of the fragrant fields
No sweeter, subtler perfume yields
Than the aroma of your breath,
Delicate fragrance attarred 'neath
The sculptured, firm, white beauty of
Your throat, arched stately there above
The undulation of your breast
That heaves with love's divine unrest.

NEAR THE END OF APRIL

NEAR the end of April,
On the verge of May —
And O my heart, the woods were dusk
At the close of day.

Half a word was spoken
Out of half a dream,
And God looked in my soul and saw
A dawn rise and gleam.

Near the end of April
Twenty Mays have met,
And half a word and half a dream
Remember and forget.

HYMN FOR THE SLAIN IN BATTLE

LORD, God of all in Life and Death,
    The winter's storm, the summer's breath,
Of fragrant bloom, — whose Mighty hand
Decrees the pow'r of sea and land,
Hear, Lord, this prayer for those who are
Slain in the hour of thund'rous war.
Have mercy, Lord, on those who fall
Rent by the iron-splintered ball.
Reck not their cause was right or wrong,
'Twas Duty led them blind and strong.
They shaped not what to war gave rise —
They make the greatest sacrifice.

A SUMMER NIGHT'S ENCHANTMENT

THE perfume of the garden blows
    Fill'd full with scent of musk and rose;
The little bay beneath us here
Is like a woman's jeweled hair,
Studded with sparkling shafts of light
Reflected from the diamond'd height.
And somewhere in the grove is heard
The passion of some love-lorn bird;
And you, my dear, beside me here
With joy around us everywhere.

IN THE HIGH HILLS

HEIGHT overhead to the deeps
    Where the gleaming day-star peeps
From the bosom of the dawn
In God's infinite blue lawn.

The wings of the winds are whirled
Over the face of the world —
And the echo of them fills
The everlasting hills.